Time Management Strategies for
Regaining Command of Your Day

PAUL H. BURTON

DONE!
Time Management Strategies for
Regaining Command of Your Day

Copyright © 2013 by Paul H. Burton

Published by:
Paul H. Burton
www.quietspacing.com

Page layout by Ad Graphics, Inc., Tulsa, OK 74145

Printed in the United States of America

ISBN 978-0-9818911-8-7

About the Author
Paul H. Burton

In past lives, Paul has been a corporate finance attorney for a law firm, a professional-services director for a software company, and a dot-com entrepreneur. Since 2005, he has been a speaker, author, trainer, and coach, working with executives and professionals who want to regain command of their day, get more done, and enjoy a greater work-life balance.

Paul was afflicted at a young age with a desire to accomplish things efficiently. At thirteen, he was tasked with the daily chore of vacuuming the family business. Paul found the most efficient route to accomplish this so he could spend more time fly-fishing.

Later, he developed a way to outline his law school courses that assured him of good grades and more time to play golf. At the software company mentioned above, he streamlined the licensing process so his contracts administrator could do most of the legal work, leaving him time to manage the professional-services department. His dot-com—Outdoorplay Inc.—does with seven employees what his competitors do with twenty.

This focus on process and individual contribution resulted in Paul's creation of the QuietSpacing time-management system and its related books, seminars, and workshops. These programs provide people with the tools they need to meet their goals of regaining command of their day, getting more done, and enjoying greater career and personal satisfaction.

Table of Contents

Introduction

The Symphony in Distraction Major

One day, on the sixteenth floor of a busy office building in Portland, Oregon, I discovered my calling. I was meeting with a client whose new e-mail alert kept dinging. Once finished glancing at it, he'd look back and say, "Sorry about that. What were you saying?" Next, the phone started ringing, causing him to look away again before he returned to me. Then somebody came to the door, interrupting us. This carnival went on for a full hour. Everything was going on, and nothing was getting done.

Somewhere during all the pinging and ringing, knocking and talking, I looked across the desk at my client. It wasn't even noon, but he looked like he was just finishing up an eighty-hour workweek. At that exact moment, I realized that we needed to *quiet* his *space* down—both his physical space and his mental space. We needed to find ways to reduce the number of interruptions and distractions he was suffering from throughout the day so that he could stay focused, get more done, and regain command of his career and his life.

I knew right then—absolutely knew—I could help him stop drowning in his noise, clutter, and chaos. I also knew that he wasn't the only one who suffered from this always-on, 24-7, 365-day world. All of us worked in this *Symphony in Distraction Major*.

I never did get to have a productive meeting with my client that crazy morning. However, after I left his office, I did a little math—math involving productivity and time management. Now math is not my strong suit, but I realized quickly that if people increased their productivity by just six minutes a day, they could regain command of their time and enjoy a greater sense of success.

You may be thinking that six minutes a day isn't much, but it adds up to twenty-four hours over the course of a year (6 minutes/day × 240 workdays/year ÷ 60 minutes/hour = 24 hours/year). That's three extra eight-hour days of work each year! Imagine how you'd feel if you had three days' worth of work off your desk right now. Wouldn't that be incredible? You'd have the proof of your success right in front of you—a cleared desk, an empty inbox, and a darkened office—because you went home earlier!

Increasing productivity is a combination of (a) managing your time better, (b) being more organized, and (c) fine-tuning workflow processes. Small improvements in each of these areas will continue to pay you productivity dividends every year. That's worth pursuing, isn't it?

I certainly thought it was on that fateful day of watching the *Symphony in Distraction Major.* I went on to create a productivity methodology called QuietSpacing®. QuietSpacing® is a systematic way to effectively process all the things coming at you during the day while reducing the number of interruptions and distractions that prevent you from being more productive.

Since 2005, I've trained and coached hundreds of people on how to incorporate the QuietSpacing® method into the way they like to work. And from all those hours of working with others, I've gathered together a series of best practices anyone can use to get their six minutes of increased productivity each day. These suggestions don't require you to learn the QuietSpacing® method, and no magic tricks are involved. These simple tips can squeeze more productivity out of the way you already work.

So if you're ready to get three days of your life back every year, let's jump in and get started. First, here's a look at how this book is organized.

In the following chapters, we will cover four focus areas. Each area will contain six suggestions, specific examples, and a smattering of client stories to help you understand the reasons behind each suggestion and how it can be applied.

But the most important thing to keep in mind while you read these tips is that we're looking for only *six minutes* of extra productivity. Just six minutes. Therefore, if you find that one or more of the suggestions doesn't apply to your situation, simply disregard it and move on to the next. These tips have all worked for someone, but not all of them will work for every individual.

The Four *DONE!* Categories Are:

E-mail

*

Schedule

*

Tasks & Projects

*

Workplace Environment

CHAPTER 1

Regaining Command of Your E-mail

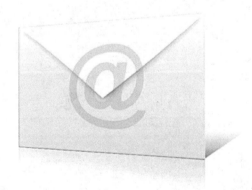

E-mail, for better or worse, is here to stay. It is the boon and the bane of our modern existence, and we have a love-hate relationship with it. Most of us claim to despise it, but few of us can go an hour without checking it.

Why this Pavlovian response exists in us is something for the psychologists to answer. Our purpose here is to find methods for dealing with e-mail more productively—in other words, to find ways to get this horse back into the barn a little more. And we'll start by tackling one of the most intrusive and distracting events that occurs dozens of times a day to each one of us . . .

1 Turn Off New Message Alerts

Were you sitting down when you read that? I hope so, because most people visibly flinch when I suggest it to them. You see, the problem is that every time a new e-mail alert pings on your computer or smartphone, you're yanked away from what you were just doing.

Poof—one e-mail and your focus is gone!

I know, I know—you can't do your job without e-mail. Of course you can't. It has become the primary form of communication worldwide, so eliminating it isn't an option. However, every time you're pulled away by a new e-mail hitting your inbox, you become increasingly unproductive.

Client Story:
Processing and Reprocessing

Several years ago, I was working with a client—Jennifer J.—to set up her Microsoft Outlook application to work a little more efficiently. I had asked her to click View on the menu bar. Just as she reached up to do so, her computer went *ping*, and the New E-mail preview flashed in the bottom-right corner of her screen. I watched her glance down to read the preview, process what it said, look back up to the menu bar in Outlook, reprocess the instruction I had just given her, and click View. It took her four seconds to do all this—I was counting in my head. This was four seconds of activity without productivity, where a lot was going on, but nothing was actually getting done.

You're saying to yourself, "Big deal" or "But it might have been important" or something

---

similar. Let's address each of these responses separately. First, four seconds may not seem like a lot, but the average corporate employee receives about one hundred e-mails per day. If we multiply a hundred by those lost four seconds, we get four hundred seconds. That's more than six and a half minutes of lost productivity per day right there! There's your six minutes. You're done. You can go home now. Thanks for playing.

Second, as it relates to whether it might have been important or not, the real answer is to find a better way of processing our e-mail to make sure we're seeing those important items in a reasonably effective manner that allows us to remain responsive to others. More on that below, but let's drive at the heart of the issue here. When the new e-mail alert sounded, was what you were doing important? Of course, we must constantly reprioritize our workload, but doing so every time an e-mail arrives is excessive. This is especially true in light of studies that suggest that it can take up to twenty minutes to get back on task once distracted (*New York Times*, "Slow Down, Brave Multitasker, and Don't Read This in Traffic," March 25, 2007).

Be brave. Take the step. Turn off the alert and remove this self-inflicted distraction. Quiet down your space by ninety-nine *pings* a day!

To address the issue raised above—that turning off the alert doesn't eliminate the need to check e-mail—let's turn to an old-school way of processing our mail . . .

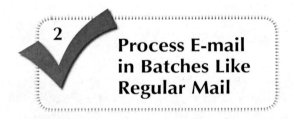

2 Process E-mail in Batches Like Regular Mail

Get outside the box—the inbox! Go to your e-mail inbox periodically throughout the day, as regularly as necessary to remain effective and responsive. Start by checking it every fifteen minutes, and then stretch it out to twenty minutes, before finally heading out to thirty minutes. Some people have even gone a whole hour without checking their e-mail. Imagine, an hour without checking e-mail!

Don't worry. No matter how long (or short) the interval is between check-ins, there will always be new e-mails to read. That's the problem with e-mails—they're constantly arriving! And if they're not, call IT, because you'll have no idea how to fix it.

Once you've arrived back at your inbox, read and sort (mentally) all the new e-mails in one continuous behavior—just like how you process your physical mail when it arrives each day. The point is that processing is a singular effort and should be started and completed in one effort to keep it most efficient.

Example:
Walk to the Mailbox

You arrive home from a long day at the office. You toss everything on the counter and go out to get the mail. When you reach the mailbox, you open it, reach inside, and grab the first item. Now you head back into the house, where you open that letter and sort it before heading back out to the mailbox for the next item.

Would you ever do that? Of course not. It's ridiculously inefficient. So why do we deal with e-mail this way? The answer is simply because we always have, not because it's the best way. That's why the solution is to adopt the old-school way of processing mail—in batches. Visit your inbox periodically, process everything that has recently arrived, and get on with the next thing you need to get done.

We've looked at a couple of ways to deal more effectively with e-mail that's coming into our inbox. Let's turn our attention to a couple of things we can do to make the e-mails we send a little more efficient.

3 Only One Subject per E-mail

Not only is putting multiple subjects into a single e-mail unnecessary—they're virtually free to send—but doing so greatly increases the risk of misunderstanding and mistakes. Consider the following example.

Example:
Story around the Campfire

Most people have camped at least once in their lives. As a result, many of you will have played this age-old camping game. While sitting around the campfire, the first person

---

whispers a story into the ear of the person next to him or her. This second person then turns and whispers the story into the ear of the third person. The process is repeated around the circle until the last person has heard the story whispered to them. That person then tells the story to the entire circle out loud, before the first tells the story he or she originally told. The differences between the two stories are always huge.

The reason for the discrepancies in the stories is that people remember only a portion of what they see, hear, and read. Consequently, when you begin to mix information related to multiple subjects in a single e-mail, you begin to risk misunderstanding and confusion on the part of the reader. And that's the least of your worries! The worst-case scenario is that your reader acts on some mix of the information contained in the e-mail, which can result in the reader actually doing the *wrong* thing. Not only can that create large problems, but it's also inefficient and ineffective, because whatever remedy must be applied is duplicated effort.

People recall things differently all the time and mix subjects up. When you commit to a one-subject-per-e-mail policy, you will increase efficiency and receive responses that make sense and are pertinent to the information you are seeking. One subject per e-mail will also provide the following benefits:

- The e-mail is easier to find later, whether through a Search function or a Sort function.
- It's easier to file.
- It reduces the risk of inadvertently disclosing sensitive or confidential information by a downstream reader looking at the content related to the other subject in a multiple-subject e-mail.

The fourth suggestion in our focus on e-mail is a complement to our third . . .

4 Craft Good Subject Lines

E-mail Subject lines are routinely underused, if not completely misused. Here are the top violations we see each day:

- [   ] (blank Subject line)
- Hey, what's up?
- I was thinking
- Urgent (or ASAP or HIGH PRIORITY!)
- Thoughts?
- Update

The beauty of the Subject field in e-mail is that it gives you an opportunity to communicate a brief sketch about what is contained in the e-mail without the recipient even having to open it. Well-crafted Subject lines tell the reader what the e-mail is about and how important it is. Moreover, they provide the same benefits listed above for the one-subject-per-e-mail suggestion:

- The e-mail is easier to find later, whether through a Search function or a Sort function.
- It's easier to file.

Example:
Morphing the Business Letter

Not so long ago, we sent letters to one an-other—in both our business and our personal lives. The business letters had a generally accepted format that looked something like this:

[Date]

[Address Block]

[Re:]

[Salutation,]

[Body]

[Signature Block]

All of these components survive in e-mail today, and all but one are used in much the same way. You've no doubt guessed that the exception is the Subject or Re: line.

In years past, the Subject line would *never* say,

Hi, how are you?

or

Update

or [   ] (blank Subject line)

It would be robust—so robust that the reader was well informed about the subject of the letter before even beginning to read, to wit:

Johnson Matter, #345365—Activities in the Last 30 Days

XXX Strategic Marketing Project—Documents for Review

You don't necessarily need to create a naming convention for Subject lines (i.e., a format for repeated use), though they help. You just need to leverage the space you have to give your reader a quick insight into the body of your e-mail.

One of the terrific side benefits to leveraging your Subject line is that everyone else will notice the change. It may take a while, but eventually, people will comment on how effective your e-mails are (especially if they contain only one subject *and* a great Subject line). That's the perfect opportunity to comment on your strategy and demonstrate true leadership—effectively getting people to do what you want them to do.

The last two tips on the following pages are uniquely separate from each other and from the ones above. The first is truly a techno tip, and the second is more of a plea, so let's jump right into the magical one . . .

5

Drag and Drop E-mail to Create New Appointments and Tasks

(Before diving in to the specifics of this suggestion, please understand that this particular tip works best with Microsoft Outlook. Other e-mail programs, such as Lotus Notes or Google Mail, have some limited ability to perform this same feat, so proceed with caution if you are using something other than Microsoft Outlook.)

Many people use e-mail to coordinate events and exchange information about tasks and projects. Many of these messages taken back and forth contain valuable information about the event or task. In order to capture that content, most people cut and paste it from the e-mail into a new appointment or task. Here's a tip that can save you quite a bit of time: Click on the e-mail with the content you need for the upcoming event or project. While you're still clicking on the e-mail, drag it over the new Appointment or Task icon (whichever is applicable to your specific application). Now release the mouse. The body of the e-mail will be automatically copied into the comment area of the new appointment or task. This is a very convenient and effective way to move information between e-mail and appointments and tasks.

A terrific application of this tip is provided by the following example: Let's say you and Beth are discussing—by e-mail—a project that you're working on together. You've been trading some ideas back and forth over the course of several messages when Beth proposes that you meet for lunch next Tuesday to nail down some specifics. You agree to a date and time via more e-mail exchanges. Now before moving on to the next task of your day, you can click and drag that e-mail down to your Appointment icon and let go of the mouse. Voila! The entire thread of your conversation now populates your new appointment. Adjust the Subject line to reflect the specifics of your upcoming lunch with Beth; set the date, time, and reminder; and click Save and Close. You can now forget about that project entirely and get on with your day.

Next Tuesday, when the reminder alerts you about your upcoming lunch with Beth, you can simply open the relevant appointment, and everything you need to review before heading off to lunch is right in front of you. No hunting around for the e-mail thread with Beth in your inbox or other storage locations. It's all right there. Note that this tip works with any kind of appointment—meetings, teleconferences, and so on—and any kind of task. Finally, once you've created the new appointment/task by dragging and dropping the original e-mail, you can file the e-mail away wherever necessary, confident that the information will be served up to you when the predetermined time arrives.

I've spoken a lot about how to handle e-mail in terms of managing the flow of messages we receive and how to be more effective with the e-mails we send. This last suggestion focuses on the volume of e-mail floating around—specifically, how to reduce the amount of e-mail that is circulating. If we could get everyone who uses e-mail to

6 Minimize the Use of Reply All

then the amount of e-mail circling the globe would diminish significantly! Reply All has become the de facto icon to hit when replying to e-mail. Based on interviews of e-mail users I've spoken with, the thought is that everyone who's on the list needs to receive the information being contributed. The second most popular reason for using Reply All is a form of covering your . . . well . . . bases.

The reality is that most people do *not* need to read the information you are contributing to the thread; only some of them do. The best practice here is to click Reply and add back *only* those people who will benefit from the information you have to contribute. This will cut down on the total number of e-mails the other people on the thread receive.

Cutting down on the number of e-mails people receive has the obvious benefit of reducing the total number of e-mails they need to process. It also means they are less likely to accidentally delete an e-mail they *do* need to read and address!

* * * * *

E-mail is communication technology that's not going away. In fact, as more and more people across the globe come to the Internet, I predict that the number of e-mails sent and received will continue to increase for some time to come. Since ignoring it isn't an option, we need to find ways to make better use of this powerful technology. Pick and choose among the six suggestions listed here to find small ways to increase your efficiency and effectiveness with this modern-day tool.

Regaining Command of Your E-mail

1. Turn off new message alerts.

2. Process e-mail in batches like regular mail.

3. Only *one* subject per e-mail.

4. Craft good subject lines.

5. Drag and drop e-mail to create new appointments and tasks.

6. Minimize the use of Reply All.

Smartphone Corner: E-mail

People often ask me how all this pertains to their use of smartphones. My response is unerringly the same: these devices are supplemental tools and *do not* replace their more advanced cousins—the laptop and desktop. Specifically, I recommend that people use their mobile device primarily for reviewing and clearing their activities. By that I mean that they review their e-mail and phone messages with a view toward clearing them off the system. Responses should be limited to short one- or two-sentence missives with specific answers or directions. I wager that no one will write the next great classic on their BlackBerry! As a final note, if a response is both (a) urgent and (b) will require more than one or two sentences to complete, try using the *phone* function to communicate directly with the other person. It's not only more efficient (as most calls of this nature can be quite short), but also more effective because you can make sure the other person understands your answer in real time.

CHAPTER 2

Regaining Command of Your Schedule

A while ago, I was watching a professional basketball game. The players were running up and down the court—dribbling, passing, shooting, blocking—and watching the defense, the shot clock, the game clock, and the coach. It was frenetic, and as the game wore on, the players became visibly more and more tired. The more I watched, the more the pattern of frantic activity seemed familiar to me until, sometime in the third quarter, it hit me. This level of activity is exactly what today's worker endures every day—running from meeting to meeting, in between conference call after conference call until, exhausted, we leave for the day. The only major differences I could discern were that professional basketball players (a) have to do it for only forty-eight minutes a game and (b) get paid millions of dollars a year!

Just as this epiphany showered me in a glow of understanding, I noticed that the home team was struggling a bit. They had slipped a few points behind, and the momentum was definitely with the opposing team. Before things got out of control, the home team coach did exactly what the first suggestion in this scheduling area recommends:

7

Schedule Time between Appointments

When we run from meeting to meeting to meeting and conference call to conference call, we become fatigued. We begin forgetting things about our last meeting as we jump into the next phone call. Whenever I see a calendar littered with back-to-back appointments, I'm put in mind of an executive rushing down the hall with pieces of paper floating to the ground in her wake. Each piece of paper represents a good idea she had in the last meeting that is now being left behind as she rushes into the next meeting.

By scheduling a short break on your calendar between meetings (five to fifteen minutes), you are able to

- record all those good ideas on paper or electronically,
- check in with your team members,
- check your messages,
- review the materials for the next meeting, and
- even take a short breather during the day!

It is often said that life is a marathon. To this I reply, horse pucky. It's a series of short sprints. We work better when we're laser focused for short periods of time and then take a break before getting back to it. In fact, many people report that they have their best ideas when they're *not* trying to have good ideas, which suggests that our minds are even more efficient when we're allowing them to rest!

For those of you who have others schedule your calendar, simply instruct them to hard-code a five-minute space after each appointment that gets scheduled. At least that way, people have to ask you if they can schedule you into that time slot. You may not get five minutes between every appointment, but even once or twice a day would be nice, wouldn't it?

To further examine this topic of calendar management, why is it that so many people put their tasks on their calendar? To me, that's just putting spaghetti onto a plate. To-dos are mixed in with appointments, with very little clarity on when your time is committed to an appointment and where you may have open time to focus on the project du jour. Consider this example . . .

Example:
The Kitchen Metaphor

Most of you have a kitchen at home. And most of you have a silverware drawer in your kitchen. Many of you have a junk drawer in that same kitchen, where you place everything for which you have no other place. Question: how many of your work calendars (electronic or otherwise) look like the junk drawer instead of the silverware drawer?

This leads to the next suggestion, which is . . .

8 **Put Appointments on the Calendar and To-Dos on a Task List**

The fundamental point here is to separate appointments from tasks so you can determine how to best allocate your time throughout the day. The human brain is very good at integrating disparate items, but it's fighting an uphill battle when it must separate the various items first. An addendum to this suggestion as it relates to calendars (especially electronic calendars) is to set the view as a series of columns (one per day), with time slots appearing vertically. This will provide you a visual display of how your appointments consume your day and where you can slot tasks into the mix.

Moving beyond the specifics of better calendar management, this next suggestion draws from ancient times (i.e., predesktop times) to leverage another benefit of the mind. For you older readers, think back . . . way back . . . to, say, 1985 . . . a time when you *did not* start your day by diving into your e-mail inbox, only to look up two hours later to wonder how all that work stacked up around you was going to get done now that half the day was gone. To wit,

9 Regularly Survey Your Landscape

Fast-forward to the present. Today, most people jump right into their e-mail and begin responding to all the messages they received overnight. W-R-O-N-G. This is the worst possible way to manage a workload. It wrongly assumes that what came in last night is more important than what's already on your plate of things to do.

There are two other mistakes being made here. First, most people make commitments in their responses to those early morning e-mails, with complete disregard for earlier commitments made to existing projects. Second, by diving right into the deep end, you are losing valuable time at the beginning of your day for planning. By the time you've run through the inbox of X dozen e-mails, that planning time is gone, and you spend the rest of the day playing catch-up.

Back in the day, we would sit down at our desks and re-view everything on our calendar and our task list and take inventory of the piles of files stacked up (tossed?) around us. Once we had surveyed the situation, we would priori-tize our work and then dig in and get to work. This review would be conducted again at midday and again at the end of the day, to fine-tune our tactical plan and to integrate any new demands for our time.

This method of surveying the workload, adjusting the plan (and the related expectations—ours and others), and then getting back to work is still a sound strategy today. The sense of urgency in our days has drawn us away from the simple truth that a little planning goes a long way toward getting more done and maintaining control over our workloads and our productivity.

Implementing this behavior is simple. Sit down at your desk, and review your calendar and task list, as well as any other items in your work area—essentially, take an inventory. Then jump into your e-mail. You'll have a better handle on where your time is committed when responding to your e-mails. Do this again at midday; the day is half over, so your ability to project what is actually going to get accomplished for the day is more accurate. Integrate any new demands on your time, adjust any deadlines that need adjusting (and communicate those changes to others who need to know), and then get back to work. Finally, at the end of the day, do a final survey. Since the day is now over, you need to adjust any remaining work with a "today" deadline to a future date and communicate that to all those concerned before going home.

Engaging in these simple surveys does wonders for your sense of command over your day. Moreover, you are more effective and responsive to others when you have a better handle on how your workload is ebbing and flowing throughout the day and adjusting accordingly. Your team members too will feel that you're more in command of your workload.

After working with thousands of people to help them gain a little more out of each day—productivity, time, accomplishment, life—I've come to one clear conclusion: we, as a species, are optimists! In the face of overwhelming evidence to the contrary, we routinely underestimate how long a task or project will take. Generally, optimism is a good thing. However, in this instance, it's not. In fact, it's a very counterproductive thing. Here's the downward spiral that results from underestimating how long a task or project will take:

Step 1: Overly optimistic commitment is made for a project's deadline.

Step 2: Stress mounts as deadline nears, and you realize you can't complete the project on time.

Step 3: Time is lost negotiating deadline extension (activity without corresponding productivity).

Step 4: Stress lingers from missed deadline and increases from knowledge that deadlines on other projects are now slipping.

How can we escape this death grip, this never-ending downward cycle? How do we manage our inner optimist?

Well, funny you should ask . . .

10

Schedule Only Four Hours of Work a Day

The primary reason we fall prey to overcommitting on deadlines is that we think we have eight hours a day to work. Of course, the reality is that we rarely have eight hours a day to work because of interruptions, meetings, and the always-present emergency du jour (something I call "getting thrown under the bus"). Yet in spite of the daily drubbing we take, we rise each day renewed like the phoenix, believing (hoping?) we'll have eight hours *today* to work.

The best way to combat this optimism is, to the extent you *can* control your schedule, to *schedule* yourself for only four hours of work time each day. Set deadlines and make commitments accordingly. The more you can do this (even if it's only once or twice a week), the more likely it is that you won't end up losing time later renegotiating a deadline extension.

Client Story:
Four Hours? I Wish!

Several years ago, I was giving a QuietSpacing® seminar and arrived at the point in the presentation where I made the "Schedule Only Four Hours of Work a Day" recommendation. Just as I finished making the statement, I heard from the back row, "Four hours? I wish!" Looking to the back of the room, I spied Eric B., an old college friend of mine, who must have sneaked in after the seminar got started.

Unable to duck the outburst in a room full of people, I forged fearfully ahead and asked Eric what he meant. Eric, never a shy person, stood up in the back and said, "I schedule my work based on a two-hour day! It's the only way I can make the deadlines I set."

With a huge sigh of relief, I thanked Eric for his participation and continued on with my explanation for how managing your available work time reduces the amount of activity with no productivity later.

No matter how much you leverage this idea of available work time, the interruptions and distractions that bombard you while you're trying to get something done can seriously hinder your productivity. The next tip helps reduce those interruptions by borrowing from another industry: teaching . . .

11 Establish Set Office Hours

Teachers and professors alike use the notion of office hours to let students know when they will be available to assist them with their questions and homework. The beauty of this system is that it forces the person with the questions to collect them and present them all at once. As a result, several things can and do happen:

1. One of the succeeding questions answers an earlier question, eliminating the need to address the first question.

2. The drop-by-and-ask-every-question-that-comes-to-mind behavior stops, reducing the number of interruptions and distractions you suffer.

3. Addressing a group of questions at once is inherent-
   ly more efficient (thank you again, Henry Ford) and
   provides an extended opportunity for learning and
   mentoring, given the longer duration of the meeting.

Many executives and professionals who work with as-
sistants engage in a once-a-day sit-down that blends the
concepts of "surveying all you command" and "schedule
set office hours" into one meeting. It's a tactical planning
session of sorts and certainly doesn't need to be limited
to these relationships.

Note that this suggestion makes team members more efficient too. When they know they will get time with you at
a specified time, they won't jump up and run to your office with every question, meaning they'll remain on task
and stay focused longer.

An Alternative to "The Doctor Is In" Model

Very early in my career, I was a newbie lawyer
at a large law firm in Portland, Oregon. One of
the partners in that firm, Jim K., was a very well-
respected, effective, and successful attorney.
One of Jim's habits was to close his door every morning from 9:00 to 11:00 a.m. so that he

could focus on the few key objectives he needed to accomplish that day. The unspoken rule
surrounding Jim's closed door was that unless
the building was on fire, you'd better not knock.
I know this because I broke the rule once. Jim
had a way of looking at you with an expression
that haunts me to this day.

The point of the story is that Jim carved out two
hours each day to get work done. He came to
the office in the morning, made or returned
calls that required his attention, spent two hours
behind his closed door, and then made and returned more calls from 11:00 a.m. until lunch.
And for those dismissing this idea as a quaint behavior from bygone days, understand that one of
the reasons Jim was one of the most respected
and successful lawyers in Portland was that he
got his work done. This is another example of the
difference between *responding* to others and being *responsive* to others.

To round out the sixth tip here in the schedule management area, let's go up a few thousand feet and look
down on ourselves. Some years ago, Deepak Chopra wrote a book called *The Seven Spiritual Laws of
Success*. In the first chapter of the book, Mr. Chopra
encourages people to spend a half hour in nature every

day. The underpinning of this suggestion is to connect with nature and the world at large, as well as to give your mind a rest during the day.

For our purposes here, the suggestion is to simply . . .

12 Take Short Breaks

Contrary to the common wisdom, this life thing is not a marathon. It's a series of short sprints. Our minds and bodies work better with regular intervals of rest. We feel it most significantly physically—we get tired, our backs hurt from sitting too long, and so on—but our minds also become less efficient when they are overtaxed. This is evidenced by our having trouble focusing on the task at hand or becoming very easily distracted.

To remedy this mental fatigue, take a short break every couple of hours. Get up. Walk around the office. If you can get outside, do so. If you can't find another way to rest your brain for a few minutes, then read the paper or seek out a colleague who's doing the same thing and chat. You'll find that upon your return, you'll be refreshed and more focused on your work. The net result is that you are more productive and less fatigued at the end of the day.

* * * * *

Modern schedules are packed full of meetings and phone calls. In the midst of this web of appointments, progress on the ever-growing mountain of tasks must be made. This chapter has covered a number of ways to organize the madness a little better to ensure that you retain your sanity in the midst of it all.

Regaining Command of Your Schedule

1. Schedule time between appointments.

2. Put appointments on the calendar and to-dos on a task list.

3. Regularly survey your landscape.

4. Schedule only four hours of work a day.

5. Establish set office hours.

6. Take short breaks.

Smartphone Corner: Scheduling

The meteoric rise of the BlackBerry in the business world, followed by the iPhone and its progeny, ushered in a whole new world of productivity as well as distraction. Revered and reviled in every household where one exists, these devices offer a panacea of opportunity for people to be more connected and to get more done. Nonetheless, the old adage is true: garbage in, garbage out.

Specifically, as this relates to schedule management, if you don't have good information on your electronic calendar, then good information can't be synced with your handheld device. Here's an example that ties together two tips:

Suppose you have an important lunch meeting on Tuesday, but that morning, other out-of-the-office meetings have you running late to the restaurant. If you've created a good Subject line for the appointment on your electronic calendar, such as

Lunch: Bob Jones—555.111.2222—Steelhead Diner—22 Pine Street then, as you're dashing across town, you could simply roll over Bob's phone number, press Send, and let him know you're running a few minutes late. No digging around for his number in Contacts, no calling the office to find his number if it's not in your Contacts list.

CHAPTER 3

Regaining Command of Your Tasks and Projects

Multitasking. That's been the aspiration of the American worker for the last decade as technology has been delivering more and more information to us faster and faster. The problem is that multitasking is not the panacea everyone hoped it would be. In fact, attempts to multitask actually reduce productivity and effectiveness. That's what current science is finding.

In early 2010, Stanford University released a study that concluded in part that people just don't multitask very well. But we don't even need to look to science to know this is true. Just ask yourself whether you've ever been in someone else's office trying to have a conversation with them while they checked their e-mail. How effective and productive was the experience? Not very, right?

The reason we don't multitask well is founded more on an economic theory called a *switch cost* than anything else. A switch cost is the cost (in this case, time) of switching between processes. That's because every time you switch between things—one task to another—it takes a moment to come up to speed on the new task before you can be productive. Thus, as you can see, the more switches that occur, the higher the cost in lost time.

Exercise:
Multitasking is Inefficient

You may not be willing to believe me. Who am I? You may even be skeptical of the Stanford study, so here's an exercise I borrowed (with changes) from Dave Crenshaw's book, *The Myth of Multitasking*.

- Find something you can time yourself with, or ask someone to time you.

- Get a blank piece of paper and a pen or pencil.

- At the top of the paper, write the word *inefficient*, which is eleven letters long.

- Underneath, create two lines of eleven dashes each, like this:

  — — — — — — — — — — —

  — — — — — — — — — — —

- In exercise one, you're going to time yourself while you start by placing the first letter of *inefficient*—an *i*—on the top line and then placing the number *1* on the bottom line

before returning to the top line to place the
n next to the *i*, and then back down to write
a *2* next to the *1*. Stop the timer when you've
spelled *inefficient* out completely on the top
line and written the numbers *1* through *11*
on the bottom line.

- Once you've made a note of the time it took
  you to do this part of the exercise, go ahead
  and set the paper up again the same way.

- This time we're going to change one rule.
  You're going to first spell out the word
  inefficient fully across the top line before
  moving to the bottom line to count out the
  numbers *1* through *11*.

- Stop the timer when you've completed
  these individual tasks.

The result is that the first exercise should take
you about 65 percent longer to complete, because you are alternating between spelling and
counting with each action you take. In the second exercise, your brain focuses entirely on
spelling until you're finished and then moves
down to counting. As a result, you incur no
switch costs along the way.

It doesn't take a psychic to tell what the first suggestion is here in the Task area . . .

13

Do One Thing at a Time

Even though this is extremely difficult to do in the modern work environment, turning off new message alerts and working behind closed doors for short periods of time greatly assists you in reducing the interruptions that litter your day. Now with a little quieter space, give yourself a leg up by trying to work on only one thing at a time, in order to eliminate any switch costs that you're adding to your day.

Trying to multitask will make you feel like you are getting more done because your activity level will be up. However, as demonstrated in the exercise above, the reality is that you aren't as productive when you are bouncing from one item to the next and back again. This is another perfect example of activity without any corresponding productivity. Attempts at multitasking create an environment where there's a lot going on, but nothing is getting done—at least not efficiently or effectively.

Limiting yourself to doing one thing at a time is the best gift you can give yourself. When you are focusing on that one thing, you will accomplish it more efficiently, and the result will be better. However, it's not always that simple, so here's another way to get a little more done each day while also feeling better about your day . . .

14 Identify Today's One Thing

There are any number of days in a week, month, year where you feel more like the ping-pong ball than the paddle. It's all you can do just to keep your head above water. The suggestions in this book will help, but the tide can rise to tsunami levels at times, and even the best of efforts can't get you ahead of the game.

A great way to squeeze a small sense of accomplishment and command out of the worst of days and weeks is to select the *one* thing you're going to get done today. Then no matter how bad the day gets, you commit to getting that one thing done. The result will be evidence of forward movement on that day, along with a greater feeling of being in control of at least part of your day.

Client Story:
The Friday File

A couple of years ago, a client asked me to work with one of their up-and-coming people. His name was Rick. Rick had all the skills to succeed at his organization; he was technically proficient and possessed an endearing and confidence-inspiring personality. However, as his responsibilities grew, he began to struggle with the workflow processing / time management aspect of his day. QuietSpacing® to the rescue!

During one of our in-office discussions, we were reviewing the method Rick used to track his physical papers and files. He opened one of his lateral file drawers and began explaining his system. As he reached the end of the drawer, he said, "This is my Friday File." That piqued my attention, so I asked what the Friday File contained. Rick explained that the Friday File contained all the professional and personal projects he had on his plate that were not time sensitive but still needed to be completed at some point.

I asked Rick how he actually managed the Friday File. He replied, "Well, I open this drawer each Friday, review the contents of this file, then close the drawer up." Translated, he looked at the list of things in the file but never actually got any of them done because he was so busy working on the exigencies of the day.

My next question was, "What do the things in the Friday File represent to you?" Rick thought for a moment and then said, "Getting these things done represents personal and professional success to me." Holy cow! Knocking these items off the to-do list represented success inside his organization and career as well as in his personal life.

That's when I suggested that Rick pull one thing from the Friday File each week and commit to getting that *one* thing done over the next week. (Note that this is a variation of the "Today's One Thing" suggestion. The adaptation was made because the items Rick was removing were larger projects, as opposed to individual tasks.)

Over the course of our coaching engagement, Rick did just that. He'd remove one thing from the Friday File each Friday and commit to getting it done by the next Friday. This worked well for him, as it gave him just one item to focus on getting done over a seven-day period.

I checked back with Rick about six months after we'd worked together and learned that not only was the *one*-thing-per-week habit still working for him but he'd been promoted! He attributed a large part of his promotion to getting these extra projects done in conjunction with his daily duties and responsibilities.

The beauty of this tip is that you can use it every day if you'd like. Each morning, pick the *one* thing that will get done today. Over time, you will leave a trail of bread crumbs of accomplishment behind you.

The previous two tips help to minimize the overwhelmed feeling that many people experience during our frenetic workdays. But how do we avoid getting into that situation in the first place? Well, one thought would be to . . .

15 **Spread Priorities Out**

"This is an ASAP!" "I need this NOW!" "Urgent, Highest Priority!" These are just some of the so-called deadlines that get thrown at you throughout the day. The fundamental problem presented here is that these deadlines lack specificity and clarity. Having searched long and hard, it can be stated without doubt that "ASAP" does not appear on any calendar published today.

This is what I call the "ASAP problem," and it, and its cousins "Urgent" and "Now," have become the default mechanism for establishing deadlines in the modern work environment. The reality is that most things aren't that urgent. In fact, in almost every instance, when you deliver this project ASAP, it will likely languish on the desk you deliver it to for days, even weeks. So it really wasn't that important.

There is another side to this problem lurking in the "best intentions" side of your personality. What I mean is that we humans are overly optimistic about many things. It's a trait that likely keeps us moving forward even in the most difficult of times. However, on a less onerous note, we also tend to overcommit as a result of this same trait. We routinely hear ourselves saying, "Sure, I can get on that right now" or "Yep, I'll get it done today." This is true even when we are setting out our own deadlines, as evidenced by thoughts like, *Need to get that done today* or *Can't forget to finish that project up by the end of business!*

The consequence of overcommitting our time is more than just the stress it induces. It's actually highly inefficient, because we then spend much of our time seeking an extension on a deadline or explaining (to ourselves and others) why something *didn't* get done by the original deadline. This is . . . wait for it . . . that's right . . . activity with no corresponding productivity!

The remedy is the same for both the ASAP problem and overly optimistic tendencies. Seek specific deadlines—dates and times—and spread them out over the course of the future accordingly. It's easier to do this with work over which you have control and harder for work being assigned to you.

However, whenever you next receive something that needs to be done ASAP, simply respond with a positive statement about the work and a query about whether "Tuesday at 3:00" would work. You'll find that by placing a specific date and time on the deadline, the work giver will begin conversing in the same fashion.

(Note that there have always been and always will be true emergencies—things that come up that need your immediate attention. However, seeking clarity and specificity on every deadline facilitates your ability to ferret out those true emergencies and allows you to respond to them accordingly.)

Working in this fashion, take all the work you have and begin breaking down the various items by days and even down to morning, midday, and afternoon if that helps. The conversation with yourself goes something like, "This pile happens on Monday, these two are Tuesday's, that's definitely a Wednesday, Thursday for sure, and this is perfect for Friday."

By establishing specific deadlines and then spreading those out over the course of the near future, you regain command of your workload. That way, when someone next approaches you with an ASAP, you can clearly and with a high degree of confidence respond to them with a specific deadline option and begin the negotiation process to fit it into your day while also responding to their needs.

A Moment of Levity, Please: The Responses We'd Like to Hear to the Dreaded ASAP Deadlines

Whenever the ASAP issues forth from those handing out assignments, here's a list of responses we'd love to hear:

- Right-o, just let me look at my calendar. Hmm, when exactly is ASAP? I'm not seeing it here . . .

- ASAP, you said? As soon as possible? Terrific. I'm leaving on my long-overdue two-week vacation in thirty minutes, so I'll get this back to you in about fifteen days.

That's as soon as possible in my world right now. How's that work for you?

- Really? ASAP? If this is that important, why is it just now being brought to my attention? (Oh, silly me, the customer/ client/boss just handed it to you too. Did you have the courage to ask them the same question?)

- Fabulous! I love having lots to do—job security, you know. Now since everything you've given me is ASAP, which one should I do first?

We can only hope.

Much of managing tasks and projects have to do with the way you interact with others during the workday, as well as the way you actually complete the work. However, there's another aspect to acquiring and maintaining focus on the task at hand. It's the insidious force of distraction, and it's something we all deal with—that little voice in our head reminding us of all the things we can't forget and need to do. It's the "Don't forget that . . ." and "Need to do that and that, oh, and that . . ." The best way to silence that whispering voice is to . . .

16 Conduct Regular Core Dumps

You have a lot of stuff in your head, and you are always thinking about it. Getting focused (and productive) is largely a function of quieting down your physical and mental space as much as possible. The idea behind a core dump is to take all the things popping up in your head and commit them to some form of record—a to-do list, an electronic task-management system, or something similar. Once your mind knows that these items have been captured, it can let go of them and turn its full attention to what needs doing right now.

Core dumps can be conducted anytime and anywhere. Whenever you find yourself repeating a series of things in your head, it's a good time to take a brief moment and core-dump that list into a permanent record. You'll be surprised by how freeing this little behavior is. The weight of the world will lift from your shoulders, and you'll be able to better focus on the "right now."

Ode to the Sticky Note

One of the most successful failures of the modern world is the sticky note. These little self-adhering pieces of paper were actually developed by 3M inadvertently when they were looking for a more substantial gluing substance. Urban legend has it that while pursuing a new adhesive, 3M scientists would apply a small dab of a test product to a piece of paper and see if the paper would stick to another object. Those that didn't were considered failures.

Somewhere along the way, someone at 3M realized that you could productize these failures into what the world today calls the sticky note.

For our purposes here, the best use of the sticky note is as a place onto which to record a core dump. It's handy, comes in numerous sizes and shapes, and can be readily available for use when stuck to any number of other things you have with you throughout the day.

For example, I travel a lot in my business. That means I'm constantly on the move between hotels, airports, client sites, taxicabs, and so on. It's not always convenient for me to create a task on my mobile device or even to access a notepad. However, I always have my wallet on me, and on the inside flap I always have a sticky note attached. That way, if something I need to remember to do pops into my head, I can pull out my wallet, flip it open, record the thought on my attached sticky note, and then put my wallet away. With the thought recorded, I can get back to focusing on what I'm doing in that moment, resting assured that I won't forget to attend to that "other thing" when the time is more appropriate.

Regular core dumps help you keep your mental space quiet. If you can keep a quiet space mentally, you will significantly increase your ability to be productive anywhere. This is because your productivity is about focus. The more focused you are, the more productive you are. Continue to look for ways to reduce the "noise" you experience throughout so that you can increase your focus.

Creating a quieter, more focused space is a lot about reducing internal and external noise, but motion also causes distraction. The eye is naturally attracted to anything that moves. As our primary sense, vision is also used to maintain a sense of command over our environment—including our work environment.

Modern technology leverages vision in an effort to increase our productivity with things like larger computer monitors, crisper mobile-device screens, and so on. But this is another example of where more isn't necessarily better, which leads to the fifth tip in this section . . .

17   Use Full Screens

The use of multiple monitors at work has become common. In fact, one of my clients had five monitors on his desk and purported to work with all of them open all the time. Even those of us without the budget or authority to command multiple monitors on our desk will have multiple windows open at any one time. Either way, this is a distraction-rich environment. Every time something changes on one monitor or window, your eye will be naturally drawn to it. This causes a distraction, however slight, that eats into your focus and productivity.

In chapter 1, we demonstrated that a simple glance to the side when a new message alert pops up (with the visual preview) can cost us up to 6.5 minutes per day of productivity. Trying to work on multiple monitors at one time or even having multiple windows visible at one time can cause the same level of distraction. The short and short of all this is that you can effectively focus on only one thing at a time, so give yourself a leg up by using full screens for computer work.

The sole exception to this rule—full screens on one monitor and eliminating the use of multiple monitors—is when you are aggregating information from multiple sources into a single source. Think of this exception as the "term paper" exception. When writing a term paper, the various source documents are researched and assembled. Then once writing has begun, those source materials are stacked up around you as you write. Using multiple monitors or partial windows on a single monitor is effective for this sort of effort.

Client Story:
On Any Sunday

Several years ago, I was conducting individual follow-up meetings with people who had attended one of my training sessions earlier in the day. As I walked around the clients' offices, I would spend thirty minutes or so with people who had asked for some additional assistance in implementing various aspects of the QuietSpacing® method.

Toward the end of the day, I walked into the office of a senior partner for this particular client. He was in a beautiful corner office with glass walls facing the bay in the distance. As I approached his desk, I saw three monitors arranged in a horseshoe fashion around his work area. On the first monitor, he had his e-mail open. The second monitor displayed an open document that he was working on. But it was his third monitor that caught my eye—it was tuned to the current playoff game!

Just as I got to his desk, he turned to me and said, "I probably shouldn't have that on with you here, huh?" Really? Ya think?

We've spent a little time now looking at how we can get our tasks and projects done more productively. The fundamental notion that we're seeking to accomplish in this tasks/projects area is to increase focus by reducing distractions. Better focus creates better productivity.

However, sometimes the tip or trick can just be a simple thing that literally gets a little more done each day. And that's where we're going to end this chapter—on one of the very best tips I've ever picked up. This came one day while having lunch with a client. During our meal we were discussing the various habits we'd each intentionally developed to meet the ever-increasing demands of our frenetic worlds. While munching on her sandwich, my client said that one of her favorite tips was to . . .

18 Do One More (Little) Thing

at the end of each day. Not a big thing and not two things. Just one *little* thing at the very end of the day. Her habit was to button everything up and get ready to go home and, before leaving the office, to do one more little thing—return a call, respond to a short e-mail, put a file folder away.

Given that we work approximately 240 days a year, she was getting 240 more little things done each year. Imagine if you got 240 more little things done this year than last year. That's a lot of little things.

* * * * *

When you take command of your daily tasks at work with a logical, methodical approach, you'll start to get more things done than ever before. Go through your tasks one at a time to complete them. While you are doing that, it is time to identify *today*'s one thing that must be done. All the other urgent matters can be spread out and prioritized throughout your day or week, depending on what their urgency truly is.

As your day moves on and new tasks get thrown your way, it is important to keep your mind focused on what you need to do. The best way to do that is to conduct a core dump of everything in your mind. Put it on a list so you can quiet down your mind and get focused on what you are taking care of at that moment. One of the best ways to remain focused is to not have multiple data sources visible when they are not part of the project you are working on. When you do, it causes distraction, and you are not giving your full attention to what is in front of you at that moment on your to-do list.

Following these tips will keep you focused and more productive. The cake will be that moment at the end of the day when you get just one more little thing done. You'll leave the office feeling good about what you've accomplished.

Regaining Command of Your Tasks and Projects

1. Do one thing at a time.

2. Identify *today's* one thing.

3. Spread priorities out.

4. Conduct regular core dumps.

5. Use full screens.

6. Do one more (little) thing.

Smartphone Corner: Tasks and Projects

Ironically, mobile devices really aren't mature enough to be major players in the completion of tasks and projects while on the move. In fact, they can create some pesky problems. Specifically, any reminders associated with a task/project can be inadvertently turned off when displayed on your mobile device. That's because the device software doesn't have a good way to make the reminder disappear without disabling it. Thus, care is recommended when dealing with electronic task lists on a mobile device.

On the other hand, there are a number of ways you can continue to be productive while away from your primary workspace. You can use e-mail and voice mail to push things along. You can create voice notes to yourself and others about things in the hopper. You can use remote-access tools to download and even edit documents in your device when there's a break in the day.

Once this area of technology matures a bit more—for example, when the tablet becomes fully functional—then mobile workers will be able to springboard their productivity even further!

CHAPTER 4

Regaining Command of Your Workplace Environment

Most of the suggestions contained in this book focus on what you, individually, can do to increase your focus, regain command of your day, and enjoy your career and personal life a little more. But most of us work in places populated by others. We interact with our colleagues and co-workers all day long. In fact, much of what we do requires that we interact and work with others. However, with this need comes a cost, a cost of interruption and distraction visited upon us regularly by the actions of others.

The simple answer to reducing those interruptions is to either (a) remove all the people from the workplace or (b) eliminate the workplace altogether. In fact, suggestions of that kind are offered by so-called futurists in their attempts to shake up the perspective of their audience (see Jason Fried's TED Conference talk titled "Why Work Doesn't Happen at Work"). Unfortunately for Mr. Fried and his ilk, eliminating the workplace won't happen anytime soon, if ever. That's because, even though there are downsides to the workplace, there are a large number of upsides. For example, people can accomplish a lot when they're physically together and working as a team. The real-time, physical nature of the workplace makes it a place where the human social animal engages with its kind, developing stronger bonds and producing collective results.

Assuming we're not going to eliminate the physical workplace for most of us anytime soon, then we need to look at ways to minimize the aspects of the physical workplace that negatively affect productivity.

Ironically, the first suggestion in this series references another self-inflicted distraction that most people are completely unaware of creating. But instead of phrasing it in the negative, let's spin it around to a positive suggestion. That is to say . . .

19   **Create a Designated Work Space**

This means create room in your work space to actually do your work. Most people have their desks—the most logical designated work space—stacked with files, strewn with pictures, covered by inboxes and outboxes, and littered with phones, monitors, keyboards, and the like. In fact, most people leave only a small space on their desks, usually right in front of their chairs, on which to actually do work!

Creating a designated work space is easy. Simply clear *everything* off your desk—the piles, the files, the pictures, the phones, the monitors, the pencils, the pens, the keyboards, the mice, everything. Make that desk look like a newborn conference room table. (Note: For now, just put all the piles and files aside. They can be filed away as archival materials or stored as ready-access materials when you finish experiencing your new designated work space.)

Now sit down at your desk, take your one thing you want to work on, place it in your designated work space, and get some work done on it. Then put that one thing away and grab the next one thing. Continue working this way into the future, and you'll find that you're much more focused on the one thing in front of you.

Why is that so? Why are you so much more focused when you have only one thing in your designated work space? The answer is surprisingly simple: peripheral vision. The human eye can see 120 degrees to either side of its focus point. Peripheral vision is a vitally important ability because it lets us see things approaching from a fairly wide angle on either side of us. This ability is something we use all the time when driving or engaging in sports or even while at rest.

Unfortunately, it's not something we can turn off. That means that while we're trying to work at that cluttered desk, we're constantly aware of all the other things in our peripheral vision. That includes all those files containing tasks and projects we also have to get done. As a consequence, we are inflicting quiet little distractions on ourselves and increasing the stress we feel. Creating a designated work space eliminates that self-induced distraction and stress.

Client Story:
How Jeff Got His Mojo Back

I was meeting with Jeff in his office after conducting a QuietSpacing® seminar earlier that day. This was a minicoaching session—just thirty minutes with each attendee—focused on getting one or two quick elements of the training from the classroom into action right away.

Jeff's desk contained a large number of neatly arranged files. On the left-top corner sat the phone. In the middle of the desk, a space of about eight by ten inches was carved out where Jeff "worked."

Sitting in his visitor's chair across the desk from him, I asked Jeff what he'd like to accomplish in our few minutes together. His response was that he wanted to find some simple ways to increase his focus so he could get more done. I suggested that we create a designated work space, to which he agreed.

I stood up and reached over to grab the first pile of files on his desk. That was a mistake. Jeff immediately leaned forward and reached for his files. Lesson learned. Never touch another guy's piles!

After we recovered from that moment, I proceeded to take all the piles and files and papers and place them at my feet—on the floor, just in front of Jeff's desk. Next, I handed Jeff one file and asked him if it was something he could work on, to which he replied, "Yes."

Jeff opened the file and began working on it. I sat back and reviewed the e-mails on my mobile device. After ten minutes or so, Jeff completed the task associated with the file and looked up at me. I asked him how the designated work space was working for him. Jeff's reply was that he hadn't been that focused on his work in fifteen years!

Peripheral vision is a very powerful thing that can easily sidetrack our best efforts at being productive. Creating a designated work space is one simple thing you can do to improve your focus and get more done. But there's another thing you can do to moderate the negative aspects of peripheral vision . . .

20 Face Away from Traffic

Disclaimer: This next suggestion is not feng shui compliant!

Most people arrange their work spaces in what I've termed the Command Central layout. If the person has an office, this means that they sit with their back to the wall/window and face the door. That's to prevent Them from getting to Me. Next, the desk is usually positioned directly in front of the person, creating yet a further barrier between Them and Me. The visitor chairs are often arranged in front of the desk, facing the person whose office is being visited. Harmless enough, right?

Wrong. This arrangement plays right into the self-inflicting distraction delivered by peripheral vision, because what does this individual do every time someone walks by? He or she looks up! That's a small distraction, but what else could happen? Eye contact! Eye contact regularly results in the passerby entering the workspace and causing a significant (and unnecessary) distraction. Note, office collegiality is a good thing, but it's a bad thing when it occurs on an impromptu basis.

Example:
An Acrobat's Nightmare

An impressive acrobatic act is one where the acrobat starts spinning plates on poles of varying heights. The acrobat starts by spinning a plate on a pole and standing the pole up. Then he or she starts the second plate on a pole before getting a third plate spinning on its pole. Eventually, there are numerous plates spinning up on their poles around the stage. The acrobat is now dashing from plate to plate, swiping his or her hand along each to keep them spinning.

Imagine if someone in the audience yelled, "Fire!" Everyone, including the acrobat, would be distracted. This momentary distraction would cause the first plate to wobble and fall to the ground. Shortly, all the plates would be crashing to the ground, and the acrobat's act would lose its value.

Working on a complex task or project is a lot like the spinning plate trick. As you dive deeper and deeper into the effort, more and more ideas relating to this piece of work get spinning in your mind. If you look up at someone walking

by your office, you might lose one of the plates. If someone walks into your office in the middle of this intense focus period, all the plates come crashing to the ground.

Maybe that's why it is often said that it can take twenty minutes to get back on task after an interruption—it can take that long to get the plates up and spinning again.

So how do you reduce or eliminate this type of interruption? You face away from traffic! Generally, this is the best office arrangement for productivity. The optimal arrangement is to move your desk against the wall such that one of your shoulders is closest to the door. That way you have to actually turn away from your work to see someone at the door. This will reduce the involuntary glancing up that occurs every time someone walks by your office. Moreover, given your new orientation to the door, people passing by will see that you're working and be less likely to interrupt you unless they really need to do so!

(Note: If you work in a cubicle, this issue generally doesn't present itself. However, if you work in an open space, you can look for other ways to orient yourself away from the majority of traffic.)

But what if you can't get people to leave you alone no matter what you do with your office arrangement, including closing the door? The best solution to solve this problem is to . . .

21 **Sequester Yourself**

If you can't get them to leave you alone, just leave them! This literally means leaving your work space and going somewhere that's quiet where no one can find you. The idea here is to get a segment of quiet time to focus on the one or two things you really need to get done. Any quiet place will do—a conference room, an empty office, a caucus room, even the local library. This generally does not mean going to a coffee shop or home, as both of those environments contain their own distractions. Here are some recommended rules for applying this suggestion:

- Take only one or two items that need your focused attention.

- Sequester works for short bursts of time—one to two hours at the outside.

- Tell no one (with the possible exception of your assistant if you have one) where you are going.

- Focus on the work you're taking and return to your work space immediately when you're finished.
- Respond to messages immediately upon your return.

Client Story:
So Close Yet So Far Away

One of my very first coaching clients was a rising star at a large Pacific Northwest law firm. Abby was on her way to making partner, and the responsibilities she was being asked to assume continued to mount. She was also the primary care provider for her two-year-old daughter, which meant that her available work hours were limited by day care schedules and the like. In short, Abby was burning the candle at both ends, and the wax in the middle was getting dangerously small.

Constant interruption was Abby's number one complaint. Just when she was getting focused and productive, someone knocked at the door. Closing the door was no help because people would knock and then immediately open it. There was no end to the stream of people barging in on Abby's efforts to get things done, to say nothing of the e-mails and phones competing for her attention.

In the middle of our conversation, the obvious hit me. When Abby had walked me back to her office from the reception area, we had passed an empty office next to hers. I asked Abby, "Is that empty office next door slated for anyone in the near future?"

Abby replied, "Not that I know of."

That's when I suggested that she sequester herself over there once or twice a day to get those critically important things done. She could just grab the file she needed to work on and head next door. She should close the door to the empty office but leave her door open so people coming by could see she wasn't there.

To say this worked brilliantly is an understatement. Over the next year, Abby billed an additional hundred hours! But just as important, she was able to get her personal life back in order so she could be the best parent she could be.

Now not all hundred hours of measured billable time was the result of sequestering alone. But it's safe to say that by literally removing herself to the other side of the common wall—a distance of about three feet—Abby was able to focus on what needed doing.

Everybody is drawn in by the appeal of getting more done in less time at work. Why? That leaves time for having a life outside of work. Just imagine how great you'll feel when you go home for the night without carrying the baggage of the office in your head. You don't have to think about all those unanswered messages and e-mails. The piles on your desk don't cast a shadow over you. When you are home, you are there not just physically but also mentally. That's what happens when you start to organize your work life. It becomes manageable.

Do everything you can, within the flexibility of your job, to get the sequestered time you need to be productive. Is there something simple you can do, like finding a vacant office or conference room? Imagine how in command you'd feel with one hundred hours of work off your desk this year. Imagine how confident others will be in you if they know you'll address their concerns and questions in a timely and effective manner. Modifying your work habits to include things like sequestering is one of the best ways to accomplish these goals.

Changing your own work habits is one way to increase your productivity and get more done, but what about the habits of others? Are there some simple ways we can help others be more productive without actually telling them what to do? The answer to that question is yes, and the first tip in helping others be more productive is to . . .

22 Elicit Versus Give Answers

Many of the interruptions and distractions we suffer from throughout the day come in the form of others asking us questions. Now when those questions are posed by our superiors or clients/customers, the right thing to do is answer them as quickly and completely as possible. However, when the questions come from our co-workers or subordinates, giving them a direct answer is often the less productive way to handle the situation.

"What?" you're saying. "Don't answer their questions?" That's right, at least not directly. You see, whenever you directly answer someone's question, what you're training them to do is ask you more questions. Wouldn't it be more effective and efficient if they could answer the questions they have themselves? Of course it would, but how can we develop that ability in others? The answer is to help your co-workers or subordinates figure the answer out for themselves.

The best way to help others answer their own queries is by asking them questions in response to their questions. The questions you ask should guide them toward the answer. This is an important distinction to draw, because it's easy to frustrate the other person when working through this process. However, when people start to have confidence in their own abilities to answer the questions that come to them in the day, several benefits result:

- They are more engaged in their work.
- They are more efficient because they don't have to get up and come to your office or type out an e-mail describing the situation.
- The number of interruptions you suffer from goes down.
- You can direct your attention to higher-value activities over the long term, because you stop answering the same question over and over; the asker has already figured out the answer.

Guiding people to the right answer involves letting them know that you will be working with them in this manner, then asking leading questions that uncover the path to the answer. When people feel like you're truly trying to help them, instead of embarrassing them for your enjoyment, they will most likely rise to the challenge simply because it's engaging. Most people want to be engaged (at work and at home), and most people want to feel like they're adding value. This is one way to accomplish this objective.

Example

Here's a quick example of the difference between giving and eliciting answers:

Question: "The X project deadline is next Thursday. Have you had a chance to review the options I sent you, and if so, which ones should we use?"

Giving Answer: "Use options two and four." Result: The subordinate has marching orders, but little application of his or her own skills and talents.

Eliciting Answer: "I've reviewed what you've sent. Which options do you feel will best accomplish the objectives of Project X?" Result: The subordinate is being asked to apply his or her skills and talent. Ownership is being transferred, which further engages the subordinate in this project and his or her job.

There's another arena where effectiveness and efficiency can be multiplied by changing your perspective only slightly: time spent in meetings. Meeting time is one of the most expensive times an organization and its people can spend. (Just think about the collective salaries sitting around the table with you!) Yet most people feel there are too many meetings and that the time they spend in meetings is unproductive. What if we were to . . .

23 Reduce Meeting Length by 25 Percent

Specifically, if you have command over the meeting schedule, reduce all sixty-minute meetings to forty-five minutes. Similarly, cut thirty-minute meetings to twenty-five minutes.

Fundamentally, work fills the time allotted. Therefore, if a meeting is scheduled for sixty minutes, by golly, it'll take sixty minutes. Cutting that same meeting to forty-five minutes requires that the work being conducted be accomplished in forty-five minutes. The underlying principle at work here is perception. If everyone walks in expecting to leave in forty-five minutes, they perceive a shorter period of time in which to work. The result is greater focus and productivity. The same is true when thirty-minute meetings are reduced to twenty-five minutes.

An added bonus can be achieved here if the next meeting is scheduled on the hour or on the half hour. That would leave either a fifteen-minute or five-minute space between meetings (*Schedule Time Between Appointments*), which allows you to check in on other projects, return some e-mails or voice mails, capture thoughts from the prior meeting, prepare for the next meeting, or maybe even relax for a few minutes!

Example:
Let Smart People Do Their Job

At one point in my career, I managed the operations for the consulting arm of a software company. Part of my responsibilities included the training department; these were the people who created and conducted the training we delivered on our software to our clients.

The two women who created the training products were both PhDs. I'm talking way smarter than me!

These employees knew what it takes many of us so long to figure out—that sitting in meetings is typically a waste of time. This is what we did. The three of us would have a weekly small round-table discussion. I'd ask them if they needed anything from me. They'd answer. Meeting done. I would go and take care of what they needed, and they'd get back to work and be completely productive in their genius sort of way.

Net result: During the three years I ran that department, we completely rebuilt our training products and doubled our training revenue. The moral of the story is that letting bright, capable people get their work done, instead of forcing them to sit through unproductive meetings, is the right thing for every manager to do!

There's another little tip you can employ to make meetings more productive and pleasant. It will take a few meetings to get this ingrained into the people with whom you meet, but if you . . .

24 **Distribute Meeting Materials in Advance**

and make clear to people that they are to review them before the meeting, you won't spend the first ten minutes of every meeting—very expensive time—repeating everything contained in the materials they have in front of them.

This is called *homework*! Remember homework? Bringing a group of people into a room to spend the first ten minutes talking to them about what you've spent hours preparing is just more time thrown away. If the materials are distributed in advance and the recipients understand it is their responsibility to review those materials before the meeting, you jump right into the meat of the value of bringing everyone into the room together—engaging in and discussing the subject matter of the meeting. This is far more productive than droning on about the materials—putting everyone to sleep or, worse, losing their attention to their BlackBerrys. The net result of shortening up the meeting length by 25 percent and distributing materials in advance makes for a more productive forty-five-minute meeting and gets people back to their other projects sooner.

Additional Suggestions for Meeting Efficiency

The examples above on making meetings more productive are the lowest-hanging fruit. However, because most workers regularly complain about meeting inefficiency, here are several more suggestions for making the meetings you hold more effective and efficient:

• Require an agenda for all meetings. The message: this is the roadmap for the discussion.

• Moderate the meeting. The message: the agenda is the roadmap to our destination; no side trips. Those are called new meetings.

• Start the meeting at the scheduled start time regardless of who's not present (including the person who scheduled the meeting). The message: meetings start on time.

• State the end time of the meeting at the beginning of the meeting. The message: this meeting *will* end on time.

- **Prohibit the use of PowerPoint or similar. The message: fancy graphics are a waste of time to prepare, a waste of time to set up, and (generally) a waste of time to present.**

- **Confirm decisions and action items. The message: this is what we agreed to do.**

- **Identify follow-up expectations. The message: this is the time line for what we agreed to do.**

Combining these simple tips and repeating them with your team will result in more productive meetings. More-over, people will feel that not only are the meetings more productive, but that they are also contributing at a higher level in the organization. This results in improved job satisfaction, greater performance, and longer retention.

So what are you waiting for?

* * * * *

Making your workplace environment a productive place is not difficult to do. It just takes the desire to do it, and you can regain command of what you have presented to you every day. Since you go to the office to work, it is very helpful to have a designated work space to actually work in. Keep it clear and clutter free.

Many times, people are drawn to us when we are working on projects and want to come in and talk. Make sure you change that around by turning your back to the door as much as possible and giving yourself sequestered time. The gift of an hour or two of quiet time a day will help catapult your productivity.

One of the most ineffective uses of time for companies and employees tends to be meetings. When meetings are scheduled, they should always have a specific agenda and purpose. If you have those things, you'll be able to reduce your meeting times by 25 percent, and that 25 percent can be devoted to your daily tasks and required follow-ups. Now that's a great way to ensure that you'll have a great workday and that you won't get derailed when you are least expecting it.

Regaining Command
of the Workplace

1. Create a designated work space.

2. Face away from traffic.

3. Sequester yourself.

4. Elicit versus give answers.

5. Reduce meeting lengths by 25 percent.

6. Distribute materials in advance.

Smartphone Corner: Workplace

The smartphone has invaded virtually every aspect of our always-connected lives. The reality is that these devices have allowed us to literally transport our workplaces to anywhere we want to transport them. This is a double-edged sword.

The ability to work anywhere allows us to make previous downtime productive. For example, leaving for the airport no longer has to be put off until the last possible minute. We can now go early and get work done while waiting our turn to board. Coincidentally, this lowers our stress level while traveling.

Conversely, checking our e-mail frequently while on a vacation negatively affects the family experience while also increasing stress. You're never actually "away" from the office.

The answer? The same as always: the smartphone is a tool. Used intelligently and in moderation, it is a positive thing. Misused or overused, it is a negative thing. Using this tool in a considered and intentional manner will deliver both increased productivity and reduced stress.

Epilogue

Distraction Major Becomes Distraction Minor

We live in a busy world. The technology explosion over the last several decades has resulted in every person being connected more readily to every other person around the globe. This ability to reach out electronically and touch the entire world is a boon for communication, commerce—the entire human race, in fact. But this benefit comes at a cost—the cost of feeling more frantic and more pressured to be responsive on a much shorter time line. Many of us feel that we have lost or are losing command of our workloads and our lives.

Regaining command is mostly about getting more focused. To get more focused, we must quiet down our spaces—work and personal. Quiet spaces are places where interruptions and distractions are reduced, if not eliminated.

This book covered twenty-four ways you can regain some command of your day and your work. Each suggestion offers a way to reduce the number of interruptions and distractions you suffer from throughout the day, as well as to help you garner that additional six-minute increment of productivity that aggregates into three days' worth of work off your desk this year.

Not every tip works for every person, but experiment to see which ones work for you. If you give yourself a chance to be a little more effective in any one of the four focus areas we discussed—

E-mail
Scheduling
Tasks
Workplace Environment

—you will find that your stress level will go down and your career satisfaction and sense of accomplishment will go up. If you give any one or more of these tips a try, you *will* increase your productivity by six minutes a day, and you *will* get twenty-four more hours of work done over the next year. If you do this, you will be left with only one question:

What Are You Going to Do with Your Three Days?

Recap of 24 Tips for
Regaining Command of Your Day

Take this page and make it into a personal checklist. When you get to work, go through each of the four areas and get yourself set up to stop the cycle of *activity with no productivity*.

E-mail:

☐ 1. Turn off new message alerts.

☐ 2. Process e-mail in batches like regular mail.

☐ 3. Limit yourself to only *one* subject per e-mail.

☐ 4. Craft good Subject lines.

☐ 5. Drag and drop e-mail to create new Appointments and Tasks.

☐ 6. Minimize the use of Reply All.

Scheduling:

☐ 7. Schedule time between appointments.

☐ 8. Put appointments on the calendar and to-dos on a task list.

☐ 9. Regularly survey your landscape.

☐ 10. Schedule only four hours of work a day.

☐ 11. Establish set office hours.

☐ 12. Take short breaks.

Tasks:

☐ 13. Do one thing at a time.

☐ 14. Identify *today's* one thing.

☐ 15. Spread priorities out.

☐ 16. Conduct regular core dumps.

☐ 17. Use full screens.

☐ 18. Do one more (little) thing.

Workplace Environment:

☐ 19. Create a designated work space.

☐ 20. Face away from traffic.

☐ 21. Sequester yourself.

☐ 22. Elicit versus give answers.

☐ 23. Reduce meeting lengths by 25 percent.

☐ 24. Distribute meeting materials in advance.